In *Prepositional* Scott Owens highlights the pr(
and with an engaging playfulness, he explore
drawing upon a rich mosaic of life experien
are a part, I am a part,/and though we can
we can never be completely apart." Brimming with artistry, Prepositional also displays our universality: "Where I come from/ is the same place you come from…" Throughout the book subtle humor abounds, bringing text and subtext into play: "Without prepositions it's hard to imagine/ where we would end up." Prepositional sweeps the reader on a rollicking journey in lyric landscapes of language, where "So much of who we are/resides there – between the lips/of any human mouth."—Ami Kaye, Publisher & Editor, Glass Lyre Press

Scott Owens writes poetry as if he were a painter, seeing more than other people see, looking beyond the obvious. Owens sees and invites the reader to visualize images, actions, beliefs, purposes, motives, and results of what he has gleaned from his life as a child, a husband, a father, a teacher, a human being who took notice.

In "Where I Come From" he explores how we are more alike than different. "On Settelmeyer Bridge," shows us that "only the names change." This is a collection of some of Owens's most loved poems mixed with newer poems such as "Coffee During Covid." Toward the end of the book, he writes about aging, what he treasures and what he has learned. In "Nearing the End of my Sentence," he writes "I long for a semi-colon, a dash, a parenthesis, at least another comma." This is another Scott Owens book I will read again and again.—Glenda Council Beall – poet, author

In *Prepositional* Scott Owens trues the lapping sand from "Where I Come From" all the way to the Dollar General where he offers the truth that words work the way they do for the enrichment of us all. We must keep on keeping on seems to be the root message, and enjoying it as we do. His philosophical lyrics prove that "Where there is language there is art."—Shelby Stephenson's recent book is *Country*. He was poet laureate of North Carolina from 2015-2018

Poet Scott Owens has been working steadily, especially in the period since 2006 on poetry that distinguishes itself craft-wise with a seamless quality that links a powerfully disturbing history to a fulfilling, successful adulthood. In *Prepositional*, he eschews the expectations for the New and Selected format by offering decidedly more of the New, a circumstance that will delight his devoted readers. If you know Scott's work, you'll know that Norman is here, of course, to direct all these flashing memories and precise observations down the forever river, "refusing to be forgotten."—Tim Peeler, author and editor

PREPOSITIONAL

Also by Scott Owens

Worlds Enough: Poems for Children (and a few grown-ups)
Sky Full of Stars and Dreaming
Counting the Ways
Down to Sleep
Thinking About the Next Big Bang in the Galaxy at the Edge of Town
To
Eye of the Beholder
Shadows Trail Them Home
For One Who Knows How to Own Land
Country Roads: Travels through Rural North Carolina
Something Knows the Moment
The Nature of Attraction
Paternity
The Fractured World
Book of Days
Deceptively Like a Sound
The Persistence of Faith

PREPOSITIONAL

New and Selected Poems

Scott Owens

REDHAWK
PUBLICATIONS

Redhawk Publications
The Catawba Valley Community College Press
2550 US Hwy 70 SE
Hickory NC 28602

ISBN: 978-1-952485-87-9

Library of Congress Number: 2022944848

Printed in the United States of America

redhawkpublications.com

Cover design by Rosemary Moua
Interior design by Rosemary Mou

DEDICATED TO

Elin
Beverly
Bud
Dennis
Mel
Nancy
Tim
Ami
Beth
Bill
Brenda
Carol
Charlie
Shelby
Dawn
Debbie
Doris
Tony
Dottie
Glenda
Carolyn
Guy
Sara
Helen
Jan
Jane
Jeff
Janice
Sue
Pat

Doug
Cory
Nikki
Betty
Jo
Karen
Kathy
Becky
Kelly
Suzy
Richard
Maren
Malaika
Margaret
Ted
Mary
Nolan
Pris
Robert
Patty
Sam
Jordan
Scott
Stacey
Damian
Keegan
Sawyer
Tina
Hannah
Julie

And everyone who has ever read a word of what I've written.

prep ·o ·si ·tion ·al

formed with or functioning as a preposition.

/ˌprepəˈziSH(ə)n(ə)l/

"the prepositional phrase "in the tunnel""

/ˌprepəˈziSH(ə)n(ə)l/

TABLE OF CONTENTS

FROM

Where I Come From.. 17
The Question of Heraldry..................................... 18
Something More 19
On Realizing the Importance of Place 20
[screen door hum]... 21
[wildflowers blooming]... 21
[field work at noon] 21
[yellow porch light] 21
[sound of night gathers]....................................... 21
The Allure of Flight... 22
On Settlemyre Bridge 23
Secrets of Southern Sweet Tea 24
Economy 25
Triptych: *Before; During; After* 27
Rosemary Is for Remembrance 29
Looking for Faces in the Night Sky..................... 30
Worlds Apart... 31
Behind.. 32
Orchard.. 33
Within 35
[among the waves] 37
Life as a Preposition.. 38

TO

[voices carry]... 42
Ways Out 43
To.. 44
13 Ways of Prepositions....................................... 45
Almost or Ode to JT O'Sullivan.......................... 48

About 49

Up 51

Upon 52

All the Difference 54

The Art of Everything 55

Towards 56

The Problem with Deciding on a Single Object to Follow the
Preposition "With" Preceding the Gerund Phrase in This
Fragment of a Title..57

Articulation 59

Words and What They Say..60

Buy This Book or A Lesson in Hermeneutics.....................61

You Do It for the Ones...63

OF

Of..66

Between..68

Yellow Xterra 69

Without 70

Of Mint and Memory 71

Communication During Covid..72

Prepositional...74

[after dawn a moment] 75

[intricate web] 75

[waxwings in treetops] 75

[reaching the river] 75

[bright morning] 75

[morning fills the ocean] 75

[waves breaking]..76

[each autumn]...76

[winter mountain drive] 76

[from this rocky perch]...76

[after heavy snow] 76

[questioning myself] 76

[how lucky the moon] 76

Water Ways 77

Another April Morning.. 78
Coffee During Covid.. 79
Reclamation 80
What's Wrong with Super Powers.......................................81

WITH

Common Ground 85
With... 86
[we planted saplings].. 87
[all the fallen] 87
Until 88
Setting the Stage 90
Naming the Stars 91
Refusing Loss 92
Relativity 93
Barrier Islands... 94
Breaking Morning.. 96
[despite everything].. 97
Out... 98
Aging Love 99

THROUGH

By 103
Wild and Precious 104
[cold December sky] 105
[there are no answers].. 105
Forward.. 106
Through 107
Keeping Pace 108
At the Reading 109
The Lost Poems... 111
Ever 112
Nearing the end of my sentence 113
All the Way Up to the Line and Beyond.............................. 115
Used 118

Into...119
[cemetery rain]...122
Epitaph...123
Away..124
About the Author...125

ACKNOWLEDGMENTS

Grateful acknowledgement is due the following journals where some of these poems were previously published.

Callused Hands for "Economy."
Charlotte Poetry Review for "Into" (as "So Norman Died Of Course").
Gean for "[How Lucky the Moon]."
A Hundred Gourds for "[morning fills the ocean]," and "[voices carry]."
Innisfree Poetry Journal for "Within" (as "Acts of Defiance").
Iodine Poetry Journal for "On Settlemyre Bridge."
The Madison Review for "The Question of Heraldry."
Mind in Motion for "Epitaph," and "Rosemary Is for Remembrance."
Red Dirt Review for "Triptych."
Rusty Truck for "[yellow porch light]," and "Yellow Xterra."
Shape of a Box for "By."
Short Poem for "Up" (as "Clark").
Side Stream for "Nearing the End of My Sentence."
Sketchbook for "[screen door hum]."
Strong Verse for "All the Difference," and "Prepositional."
Tertulia for "Relativity."
Vox Poetica for "Ever," "Keeping Pace, "Reclamation," "Towards" (as "Towards a Poetics of Excess"), and "Used."
Waterways for "Behind," and "Refusing Loss."
Willows Wept Review for "Barrier Islands," and "[bright morning]."
Your Daily Poem for "Words and What They Say."

"About," and "All the Way Up to the Line and Beyond" were previously published in *Counting the Ways* (Main Street Rag, 2020).

"Breaking Morning," "Refusing Loss," "Relativity," "Towards" (as "Towards a Poetics of Excess"), "Until," and "With" (as "How to Live a Long Time Together") were previously published in *Eye of the Beholder* (Main Street Rag, 2013)

"Rosemary Is for Remembrance," "[screen door hum]" and "Within" (as "Acts of Defiance") were first published in *For One Who Knows How to Own Land* (FutureCycle, 2011).

"Into" (as "So Norman Died Of Course") was first published in *The Fractured World* (Main Street Rag, 2008).

"By" was previously published in *Paternity* (Main Street Rag, 2010).

"Common Ground," "Looking for Faces in the Night Sky," and "Nearing the End of My Sentence" were previously published in *Something Knows the Moment* (Main Street Rag, 2011).

"All the Way Up to the Line and Beyond," "Away" (as "Denouement"), "Ever," "Keeping Pace," "Reclamation," "Through," and "Used" were previously published in *Thinking About the Next Big Bang in the Galaxy at the Edge of Town* (Main Street Rag, 2015).

"Epitaph," "Of," "To," "Up" (as "Clark"), "Ways Out," and "You Do It for the Ones" were previously published in *To* (Main Street Rag, 2014).

"[after dawn a moment]," "Keeping Pace," "Words and What They Say" and "Yellow Xterra" were previously published in *Sky Full of Stars and Dreaming* (Red Hawk, 2021).

FROM

prep ·o ·si ·tion ·al

Where I Come From

My people are sandlappers,
farmers, quarryhands, millworkers,
lintheads, rednecks, chicken chasers,
fencemenders, featherheads, post hole diggers,
gravel crushers, housecleaners, dropouts,
racists, cooks, flower gardeners,
name changers, knuckle bumpers, fistfighters,
abusers and abused, defined by
the people they cling to,
zealots, Baptists, Jews,
converts, atheists, agnostics,
Unitarians, Democrats, recidivists,
tree climbers, sandal wearers, free thinkers
hicks, hacks, hikers, and haymakers,
rock climbers, plane jumpers, whitewater rafters,
fishers, hunters, plumbers,
sons, daughters, orphans,
Scots, Welsh, Cherokee,
drinkers, divorcees, widows,
writers, poets, complainers,
soldiers, actors, Shakespeare teachers,
students, consumers, conservationists,
activists, instigators, ne'er-do-wells,
polio survivors, schizophrenics,
existentialists, optimists, organizers,
whistle blowers, finger pointers, and drummers.
All of them are all of me.
Where I come from
is the same place you come from;
my people the same as yours.
As you are a part, I am a part,
and though we can be just one,
we can never be completely apart.

The Question of Heraldry

I've decided the hawkers are right,
the ones who find your royal lineage
for a price. I mean how could any family
have had the misfortune to sleep year
after year, generation after generation,
century after century, with the farmer's daughter,
the mechanic's son? Somewhere along the line
you have to believe your father's father's
father's father found his princess,
if only for a night. I mean bad families
are bad enough to wear themselves out
after four or five generations of feuds,
stupidity, sleeping with kin. And the fact
that anyone's direct ancestors outnumber
the world population with only six or seven
centuries of counting makes any claim
of distant blue blood undeniable. After all,
here we all are, having survived this far,
and every one of us has the aunt whose red hair
has never been wholly explained.

Something More

Underaged, single mother of four,
working, stuffing underwear
into boxes, 8th grade education,
pretty face leading mostly to trouble,
hardly aware how she got there,
knowing just enough to do as right
as she knows for those she brings with her.

She saved from every paycheck
a silver dollar in a babyfood jar,
one for each child once a month
so that on birthdays they could have
something more than usual, cake
or ice cream, candy or toy, just some
little thing to make the day stand out.

And her second son understood
and later, began saving the day
his daughter was born, silver dollars,
50 cent pieces, wheat pennies,
Mercury dimes, 2 dollar bills
until there was enough to help her
do what he had had to do alone.
Get away, pay for books, school,
travel, the opportunity to know
something more than he had known.

On Realizing the Importance of Place

This is a place you think
that hardly matters,
red hill, white trailer
dog behind one wheel,
small boy, pale skin,
paler hair,
eyes blue as ice,
shoveling dirt tirelessly
with the scoop end
of a toy front loader
back and forth until
he's scooped out
a smooth bowl of dirt
redder than the earth
around it, smoother
than skin, eyes, ice and then
you realize your mistake:
that every place matters
to someone, the sunset,
the trees, the silence
of birds gliding above,
the perfection belied
by imperfect vision.
It all matters to whatever
child knows this as home.

screen door hum
of unseen cicada
as if heat could sing

wildflowers blooming
the tractor stops
a moment

fieldwork at noon
hawk hunting above
a lonely shadow

yellow porch light
flickering in darkness
swirl of candle bats

sound of night gathers
at the open window
whippoorwill

The Allure of Flight

We have all been him,
head bent, legs pumping,
swinging out and back
farther and higher each time,
if not on this mountain,
this curve of land, then another,
enjoying the flight,
temporary denial of gravity.
And we have all dreamed
the same dream,
letting go,
rising above
what holds us down,
going beyond
such mundane limitations
as earth, stone, mere contemplation,
free to see and be something more,
bird, mist, wind, star,
whatever might rise
without coming down.

On Settlemyre Bridge

On Settlemyre Bridge a boy drops a line
into water running below, the silver sides
of fish flashing as they surf eddies
standing still behind rocks as old as time.

On Settlemyre Bridge, beyond the shade
of ancient trees, a girl leans into a boy's arms
and laughs a little laugh at almost anything
he says, her face too bright to ever fade.

On Settlemyre Bridge the sun casts autumn light
through trees barely bare, littering the ground
with rustling shapes of the past year, expanding
the sky and bringing forgotten visions to sight.

On Settlemyre Bridge the land fans out
to either side, rising quickly to hills
decked with houses old and new, weathered
walls testimony to constant conquest of doubt.

On Settlemyre Bridge only the names change.
Another boy stands where time stands still,
casting bait, dreaming of water running
to places he's never seen, but never seem out of range.

Secrets of Southern Sweet Tea

Everyone who came to eat at my grandmother's house
had to answer the same question before they were served,
Jaunt drank or jaunt tay?
Drank being whatever soda was in the fridge at the time,
usually whatever had been on sale at the Bi-Lo that week,
and *tay* being tea, but not just any old tea,
my grandmother's sweet, Southern iced tea,
and anyone who knew anything about my grandmother
would loosen their belts and answer *Tay*.
Twice as strong as the box called for,
a pinch of baking soda added while steeping,
at least a cup of sugar per gallon,
tea bags finally removed, and let drip
in the pot but not squeezed,
then the whole thing poured into gallon mason jars
and chilled in the fridge for at least four hours
but preferably overnight. Served in tall, thick-sided glasses
with lots of ice (made this strong, extra ice could never hurt it).
I would add that you should never keep it for more than a week
but when it tasted as good as hers that was never a concern.

Economy

In my grandma's worldview
there were only six kinds of birds,
most simply named by color:
bluebird and yellowbird, blackbird
and brown, redbird, and buzzard.

When I asked her about the birds
I'd seen that were purple or green
or orange, she said anyone
who looked at birds that close
had too much time on their hands.

An accidental conservationist,
she was just as frugal with containers
as she was with words, every glass
a jelly jar, bread bags, and coffee cans,
foil and feedsacks always emptied
and saved, rinsed out, and reused.

At meals, too, little was wasted.
We ate the sweetbreads of animals,
the fancy parts, livers, and hearts
ground or fried pressed into loaves
and baked. Even chicken bones
were crushed and buried in the garden.

All scraps were saved for the dogs,
scraped into the bowl by the sink
and set out at dusk. Only eggshells,
corn husks, potato skins were thrown
over the fence for cows and chickens
or any of the six birds she named.

She never bought a new piece of furniture.
Everything, she said, could be repaired
or covered. She used the same beds
her family had owned before her, and we slept
two boys each in two single beds,
back-to-back and feet to head.

Clothes, too, were passed from one
generation to the next. Hand-me-downs
never so worn they couldn't be mended
or patched or at last stitched into quilts
whose squares felt as familiar
as anything saved from oblivion.

Triptych

Before

Before the light,
the whippoorwill
wakens, sings in the dark
trees, among the leaves,
around the houses still
beneath the veil of morning.

During

Purple sky dissolves to blue.
Steam rises from fields
like ghosts of what has been planted.
Smell of new mown hay
greets the day's rising.
A meadowlark calls
from a brown fencepost,
black collar against a yellow field.
A door opens, seed clatters
in a metal bucket.

After

Still cold smell of morning
hangs heavy in the air.
Trembling leaves open
to light, invite what warmth will come,
shake off the dolor of night.
Boots plod through clods of earth.

A wood thrush, hidden
among blossoming dogwoods,
sends out his song, resounding
through farm and village
and a thousand years
of furrowed fields.

Rosemary Is for Remembrance

Memory is always
the last to go,
waiting for the passing
of voices and words,
the selling or throwing away
of clothes and boxes of goods,
waiting for pictures to fade,
faces to change,
dates to be forgotten.

I missed your funeral
and I never visit your grave,
but when I go home
I pull weeds from your garden.

I remember your face
was not made of stone,
and your hands,
etched with earth,
were nothing like angels.

Looking for Faces in the Night Sky

These are things anyone could have made
up. The stars are nothing but stars,
and playing dot-to-dot in the night
sky makes anything possible.
Years ago, from the stone porch
my grandfather pointed them out:
the lion, the great bear, the hunter's sword.
This one he called Mary and showed me
how the stars made a woman's face.

Looking for faces in the night sky
we string stars into shapes of things
we fear or long to remember.
I see spider, sparrowhawk, bobwhite.
This one I'll call woman becoming
an angel, the grotesque buds of wings
sprouting in her back.

Worlds Apart

If I could speak to you
in words you could understand
I would tell you
nothing stays clean here
or unbruised, no face
can remain unblemished
by time, struggle,
all that rises against us.

I would tell you
although you find me
curious, exotic,
unusual, and hold
the lens between us,

we are not so different
after all
we dance the same,
laugh the same,
seek warmth, comfort,
escape from pain.

No matter who you are,
who you think me to be,
I will look you in the eye
and tell you
we cast the same
shadow, harbor
the same dream.

Behind

Hour after hour this ancient bed
surrenders a bounty of lily, daffodil,
periwinkle, gifts of a gardener
long forgotten, given to children
not his own, digging, exclaiming
tuber and seed.

I imagine his back bending and rising,
year after year, thinning and spreading,
claiming another piece of yard
from the obscurity of no definition,
leaving this legacy of growth
beyond years, beyond the reach
of knowing, where all that's left
is what is left behind.

Orchard

Six children play in
a copse of hollies, careless of
prickers, they feel on
their skin, pushing through
thick-leafed limbs to
find a higher perch from

which to see below. A boy swings from
a weathered rope hanging in
a sycamore tree, dropping to
cool water running below, remnant of
a river that once passed through
here even before these trees grew on

narrowed banks. Bulging fruit hangs on
limbs bent low from
harvest weight, tastes sweetened through
summer sun, ripened in
waiting. We take more than our share of
such gifts, raise each bite to

our mouths, relish in work consigned to
trees. Who hasn't dreamed of living on
limbs perched high in trunks of
trees? Possibilities we never descend from
but keep forever locked in
the backs of minds to get us through

hard times. Every place that memory wanders through

is populated by limbs to hang onto,
hidden boughs to rest in
when there's no one else to count on
and little certainty of where we're from,
as if the whole world might be made of

trees. Observing, I am reminded of
my own time climbing through
one maze of limbs after another, hanging from
thin branches of pines growing to
the sky, it seemed, holding on
to dreams, this life was born in.

Trees are worlds in which children play, heedless of
the insecurity they balance on, obscurity they swing through,
impossibility they aspire to and stubbornly rise up from.

Within

Just a boy,
not yet eight,
and knowing nothing
of the world,
I simply did as I was told
and reached my hands,
my forearms, long and thin,
even up to the elbows,
into the bloody back end
of a moaning cow
to grasp what I felt there
and pull,
and pull harder
when it wouldn't come
until something appeared,
and pull harder still
until something became
a wet mess of calf
spilling into my lap
and my uncles laughing
and my grandfather,
his hand on my shoulder,
looking at me hard,
eyes full of seriousness
saying, *Good job.*
Good job.

A lifetime later,

at forty-one,
holding you
I finally understand
the weight of it all.
I look at your mother
spent in bed
and say, *Good job*,
and then into your own
uncomprehending,
just born eyes
and say again,
Good job.

among the waves we
recognize ourselves, recall
from this we arose

Life as a Preposition

I was born from
brought into
raised by
mostly did without
left behind
looked over
steeped in
reminded of
shouted at
held back
kept under
until I

woke up
wandered off
looked around
read about
sought for
found out
set my mind to
moved out
went among
got along
fooled around
got lost in
slipped down
wound up with
but

never gave up

fought against
figured out
rose above
wrote about
went on and on
moved beyond
kept on
until I

got to
looked upon
decided on
worked at
became like
was happy with
after which
I never looked back

/ˌprepəˈziSH(ə)n(ə)l/

TO

voices carry
from faces unseen —
stones skipped across water

Ways Out

Maurice Sendak has died.
It seems absurd to say so.
Nights beneath the covers,

flashlight on,
dreaming pages to life
or a supper still hot
on the table.

How could anything as simple as death
hope to hold one who knowingly goes
where the wild things are.

To

Direction is only part,

and the smallest,

means, destination,

facilitation,

not where so much as how,

to see, to think,

to believe, to feel,

to appreciate, to do,

to be here, now,

to know, to love,

to remember,

and by remembering,

to save.

13 Ways of Prepositions

The very term denies definition.
Mr. Knudsen, in seventh grade, said,
Every way a squirrel could be
in relation to a tree and I immediately asked
how a squirrel could be through a tree
or of a tree, and I couldn't see
how a squirrel was anything like a tree.

Another teacher explained a preposition
is not a word you should end a sentence with.
The irony from such a source one of the thousand
natural shocks my flesh was made heir to.

And when I brought her, *What did you bring that book*
that I don't want to be read to out of up for?
She replied, *Ending a sentence with five prepositions*
is just the sort of nonsense up with which I will not put.

Prepositions are always different
from other parts of speech but also
often different than you thought they were.

Even though I knew it was incorrect,
I was more afraid when the bull ran at me
than when it ran towards me.

And a subtle shift in two or three
letter words can wholly change the meaning.
After all, hospitality is present
when something happens for you,
absent when the same thing happens to you.

And the same house is certainly nice
if it's the one you're moving into,
but less so if the one you're moving out of.

And I understand that while
I can stand in a field of corn,
while playing football, I stand on the field.
And, of course, while we tend to sit
in a chair, we prefer to sit on the couch.

In poems we often toss out articles,
throw away conjunctions,
all the small words we use in prose,
but we can never let go of prepositions.

Everyone told her to get over it,
work through it, talk it out.
As if prepositions could protect her. *

A preposition is a word that shows a relationship
between its object and another word in the sentence.
Relationship being that of
location: *under your bootsoles;*
time: *before my pen has gleaned my teeming brain;*
possession: *of love's austere and lonely offices;*
movement: *into the place where the answers are kept;*
manner: *like a squirrel;*
measure: *for most this amazing day;*
source: *with wine, with poetry, or with virtue;*
or agency: *with your one wild and precious life.*

Without prepositions, where could we go?

When would we get there?
How would we travel?
And would we always be alone?
Without prepositions it's hard to imagine
where we would end up.

Up, up, and away,
to infinity and beyond.

(*Sara Sligar)

Almost
or
Ode to JT O'Sullivan

You inspire us, JT O'Sullivan,
understudies, stand ins,
second-rate poets, career minor leaguers,
Hollywood extras, perennial bridesmaids,
VPs whose POTUS was never
impeached, assassinated, or just found dead.

Your example shows us it's okay
to be second, even third best,
runner-up, wait-listed, honorable mention,
fill-in, proxy, alternate,
substitute, surrogate, last resort.

You help us keep on keeping on.
More importantly, you keep us
from going insane from anonymity,
falling into depths of despair,
drinking ourselves to death.

Your 13 years of being
the 91st best quarterback in the world
reminds us if we want it bad
enough, if we just keep trying,
if the fates create just enough attrition,
we too can be third string,
almost famous, almost
what we always wanted to be.

About

Poetry is all about fun
or memory
or making things better
or seeing how one thing matters to another.

Poetry is all about making sense,
lifting veils,
drawing curtains
closed before us.

Poetry is all about using words
you could never use anywhere else:
likened, accosted, hovel, anything in Latin.

Poetry is all about making shit up:
a 14th colony,
the voice of Michelangelo's David,
the smell of scrolls burning in the Library at Alexandria,
how Lewis met Clark.

Poetry is all about engineering
a defense against the engineers.

Poetry is all about getting somewhere
especially when you don't know where that is.

Sometimes poetry is all about scaring people.
Sometimes poetry is all about making people smile.
Sometimes poetry wonders if there is any difference.

Poetry is all about writing your name

into something more permanent
than the sky outside the window right now.
Poetry can be about making lists:
reasons for living,
words worth keeping,
13 ways of anything.

Poetry is all about the riprap of things,
balance of stone upon stone,
staring into the forest at night,
walking north between the rails,
weather gathered around you.

Poetry is all about the difference
between am
and whatever is left.

Poetry is all about refusing
to be forgotten, refusing
to admit loss, refusing
to succumb, refusing
to let go easy.

If you listen closely, poetry
is all about the sounds of silence
between the words, lines, stanzas,
breaths.

Up

Up, up, and away, he said,
meaning the floor of our ceiling,
the ceiling of our floor, meaning,
if anything, everything
that boxes in, boxes out,
constricts, constrains, encloses, controls,
says, *No,* to the imagination's
tongue screaming, *Here he comes*
to save the day, like a bird, like a plane,
like anyman with his hands out
before him, his red cape blowing,
unconcealing his bright, shining S.

Upon

Which coffee I like,
Costa Rican, Ethiopian,
Brazil Bobolink, or maybe
a maple nut latte, a nitro
cold brew with vanilla cold foam
has to do with
what day it is,
what time of day,
the weather,
or how people have treated me.

Which music I choose
whether it's blues
or something smooth and dreamy
is based on my mood
or what I'm trying to do
or what urges I need to subdue.

What something means,
if it means,
is subject to
whom you ask,
where they stand,
what they expected or believed,
the angle of light,
view, or origin.

Less a theory than a fact,

everything depends
on priorities,
mood,
attitude,
time,
money,
definition,

the way you look at it,
fate, God,
you, this,
everything else.

All the Difference

Everything would have been different
if the trees had been evergreens,
if the wind had blown more leaves away,
if there had been more walkers
or the walkers had weighed more
or less if I had thought then
what worked for them might work for you,
if I had known less
of how way leads on to way,
if I hadn't read Thoreau,
if my mother hadn't been full of regret,
if the day had been brighter or shorter,
or the time sooner if there had been
even a single bird or squirrel
or the hint of anything moving in the distance,
if I had taken the other as just
as fair, or not stood as long
looking to where it bent in the undergrowth,
if I had worried about what ticks
there might be in tall grass.
Everything would have been different
if anything had been different at all.

The Art of Everything

It's not just pushing the pile along,

running hot water over grounds.

There is crema, and body, and heart.

There is working with the wind,

finding the angle that keeps the pile together.

There is knowing where to break

the line to suspend thought, breath,

create an expectation that satisfies.

It's doing whatever you do

in a way that brings out the best,

that brings out the sublime,

in the way of the studied and practiced.

Where there is language there is art.

Towards

What we need are more
words, longer
lines, stanzas that
run over, images that
pile on without pity or mercy,
poems that shrink from nothing,
poems that refuse consideration
of politics, correctness, or caution,
poems ripe with intention
and ready to burst.

Who wants to read anything
on the head of a pin?
Why choose
when you can keep it all?

Say I came to a cliff.
Say the air fell off into nothingness.
Say the past pushed me to the edge.
Say there was no turning back.
Say I couldn't resist any more than you
and all I had to walk on
were the words that fell from my mouth.

Who wouldn't want a poem of excess,
one that leaves you almost exhausted,
tongue-tied and dripping sweat,
gasping for breath, for words, for anything
that might make a single moment more of meaning?

The Problem with Deciding on a Single Object to Follow the Preposition "With" Preceding the Gerund Phrase in This Fragment of a Title

is, of course, that there are too many problems
to choose from – the war, Covid, the internet,
lives that matter, misogyny, pronouns, rockets,
the cost of health care, continued hostilities everywhere,
apathy, lethargy, global warming,
intolerance, food allergies, teen pregnancy,
the mysterious lump in the thumb of my left hand,
April, holidays, coming home, forgiveness,
the lack of forgiveness, plagiarism, flattery,
the lack of originality or sincerity or sensitivity
or giving a shit, and giving a shit,
sibling rivalry, being a superhero, domestic or otherwise,
family, closets, cats, waiting, the woman
at the Washington Zoo, the tourist from Syracuse,
Chicago, Afghanistan, who's next, me,
Gordon Ramsay, husbands, wives, fingernails,
Van Gogh's ear, the best minds of my generation,
unrequited love, requited love, success, failure,
expectations, being alive and on the Earth,
rabbits, poetry, blind dates, invented forms,
formlessness, less, more, not enough,
superfluity, Darwin, ubiquity, time,
youth, growth, a comfortable couch
with just enough pillows and the perfect end
table for holding snacks and remote,
fireflies, spring, being here,
theories of being, theories of meaning,

theories of purpose, function or form,
the inevitability of inadequacy, the inevitability
of disappointment, obsession, surrender,
waking to sleep, leaving things whole, change,
the way the world ends,
whatever way that is,
what comes next.

Articulation

Mother and daughter
in a waiting room.
From the mother's mouth,

love and warmth,
from the daughter's, curiosity,
uncertainty, sounding the depths.

So much of who we are
resides there – between the lips
of any human mouth.

Words and What They Say

Some say you can't tell anything
from the language that people use,
that Eskimos in fact have no
more words for snow than we,
nor Anglo-Saxons more
for cut, stab, thrust,
and the fact that our words for animals
when we eat them, *beef, pork,*
poultry, all come from French
doesn't prove they're better
cooks or bigger carnivores,
any more than 23 acronyms
for laughter shows that texting
teens just want to have fun,
but when I hear my carful of 2nd graders
from Sandy Ford Montessori School
making up names for the sun,
and the moon, and the stars that only
come out when you're camping and the fire
goes out, and you turn off your flashlights
while your mother holds you in her arms,
I can't help but believe
that not only is there hope for us all
but that the hope we have
is strongest when we find a way
to put it into words.

Buy This Book
or
A Lesson in Hermeneutics

Buy this book
      the book jacket said
      as if it had something to say
          (and why not)
What else
          should it/you do
Open your mind
Consider
      the possibilities
You may be changed
      B(u)y it
Suspend
          your disbelief
                         willingly
Read
                         critically
Read
          with intention
Intend
          to be b(u)y being
Reading
          b(u)y making
                         meaning

Read

to   broaden
your world
                       lengthen
your life
                       see
what you see
                        feel
what you feel
                       know
what you know
make things   mean
something

Buy this book
                or any book for that matter
Join the conversation
                Weigh in so that you
                                    matter
                in the making of meaning
                out of   matter

You Do It for the Ones

You do it for the ones,
not for the millions
you know need it
but might never be reached.

You do it for the ones,
not for the thousands
who won't be moved,
minds already made up,
wrapped tight in one
ideology or another.

You do it for the ones,
not for the hundreds
who only think
of the next game, show, drink,
other briefly pleasing distraction.

You do it for the ones,
not for the dozens
who don't care,
guided by smaller gods,
greed, anger, fear.

You do it for the ones,
with round eyes
and open mouths,
who find themselves before you,
no matter how they got there,
what shape they're in when they arrive.

You do it for the ones,

even when you can't tell
which ones they are,
even when they don't appear
to be listening because years later
they might remember
that somewhere someone
once said they were worth it.

OF

Of

Poetry is contrary to productivity.
Poetry encourages idleness.
Poetry stands at the window
because it is curious about the flowers,
this flower with its yellow fringed face
around its one brown eye.
Poetry stands at the window
because it is curious about the trees,
this tree with heart-shaped leaves,
some turning yellow in the first
days of fall, some fallen off and still
the limbs reaching up to the sky.
Poetry stands at the window
because it is curious about the sky,
how it got there, where it goes,
what it's like where it ends.
Poetry wants the window down.
Poetry walks back and forth
through a field going nowhere.
Poetry thinks it's okay to look
at the same sky day after day,
sometimes minutes at a time,
sometimes with no other purpose
but remembering blue.

Poetry refuses to follow the rules
of efficiency: *get in line,*
speak only when spoken to,
never say anything that would embarrass your mother.

The first poem ever written was a drum.
The first poem ever written was a foot
tapping on the side of the crib.
The first poem ever written was a rope
slapping the red clay playground
of William Blake Elementary School.

It is not necessary for poetry
to be beautiful
though sometimes it is.
It is not required of poetry
that it be profound
though it rarely closes its eyes.
It is not expected that the face
of poetry be etched with tears,
the hair dripping with sweat,
the mouth expressing awe.
Poetry owes nothing to anyone.

Still, poetry wakes up each morning,
walks to the edge of the world
and jumps, believing one time
it will fly, believing one time
the dive will not end, believing one time
an answer will rise from somewhere beyond.

Between

If you breathe slowly

you can see the space

between the trees.

If you leave your phone behind

each limb will reach

clear before your eyes.

If you take off your shoes

the sky will shine

behind the leaves.

If you think only of trees

you will run almost

without touching the ground.

Yellow Xterra

With the rear seat folded up
he could just fit stretched out
in the back of the yellow Xterra,
but he was exceedingly happy that
with the rear seat folded up
he could just fit stretched out
in the back of the yellow Xterra.

Through tinted glass he saw
a perfect sky of stars,
broken only by shapes of leaves,
knew the quiet of solitude,
absence of expectation.

The problem with desire, he said,
is the unlikelihood of satisfaction.

Without

Floating,
face down,
surrounded by blue,
almost becoming blue myself,

void of sound or smell,
taste or thought,
released from all but sight
and coolness of water.

Waves,
Cades Cove, Green Knob Trail,
in all the places I long to be
it is absence that drives desire.

Of Mint and Memory

The smell of mint makes everything feel clean,
clears the senses like bells ringing,
or windchimes, maybe, on a summer day
in 1973, after the war but before
the bomb became too real a thing to ignore.

They say that smell is our most powerful sense,
not the strongest, not the one
we use the most, but the one we find
closest to memory and feeling, the one
most difficult to ignore, resist, overcome.

I've given up patches of my yard to mint
so I'll always have it for tea,
for homemade chocolate chip ice cream,
for the times I need to go back to days
when I didn't know enough to be afraid.

Communication During Covid

We do our best, muttering
through masks and plexiglass.
No more reading lips,
no more touch or personal space.
We never knew how much
we depended on them.

You say, *How have you been this morning?*
And I hear, *How do you bend this woman?*
You say, *I feel like I've been working forever,*
And I hear, *I fear that I've been looking like Elvis.*

We make out a word or two,
guess the rest as best
we can from expectations,
experience, past history,
a list of possibilities
we carry in our head.

You say, *He has a PhD,*
but I hear, *He has PTSD.*
You say, *You can take off your mask,*
but I hear, *You've got cake on your ass.*

We learn to pay more attention
to the eyes, always the window
to the soul, now the sole
element of facial expression.

You say, *I think it's an evergreen,*
but I hear, *It seems we can never agree.*
You say, *You are my heart flower,*
but I hear, *You are late by a half hour.*

Usually it's harmless,
sometimes funny.
Much of it makes
no sense at all.

You say, *Poultry is reared all over the world,*
and I hear, *Poetry is read while Rover is whirled.*
Your, *Just a small coffee*
becomes, *Justice mall awfully.*

But there is always the prospect
of danger in what we hear
in our own muffled heads.

I say, *I put my heart in your hand,*
but you hear, *What you want is too hard to demand.*
You say, *We've got to get away.*
But I hear, *We gave our God away.*

Prepositional

I had not thought to see
cedar waxwings in a greening tree
along the tracks in downtown
Blue Ridge, GA, with the sun
rising from mountains behind them
to the top of a clear blue sky
on a warm morning in early April,
but once placed so undeniably
before me, how could I help
but keep my eyes upon them.

after dawn a moment
of stillness — everything
catches its breath

        intricate web —
        my eyes
        among its prey

                waxwings in treetops
                spring limb to limb —
                things begin to open

reaching the river
storm clouds shatter —
how wise old wives

        bright morning
        after three days of rain
        even the sky opens

                morning fills the ocean —
                fear not the only thing
                that makes us tremble

waves breaking —
the color blue
unfurls

each autumn
the maple tree becomes
living flame

winter mountain drive
full of sky
and empty trees

from this rocky perch
blackbird counts twenty
peaks endless blue of sky

after heavy snow
silence

questioning myself
I stop at the pond
to listen to frogs

how lucky the moon
just the right size for this
eclipse

Water Ways

Lake Harding, I've seen your islands,
Two Tree, Rainbow,
Bootleg, Chimney,
and know what it means
to be a part of
by being apart from.

I've watched your wind
blow winged cinders
of chimney swift, nuthatch,
cormorant, and osprey
in blurred flight over water,
and know what it means
to get back on course
by being blown off.

I've seen your coves and slues,
tucked away behind every curve
of land, lake water quietly lapping,
and know how it feels
to find belonging
in being alone.

I've heard your oldest names,
Halawakee, Chattahoochee,
Osanippa, and understood
the difference that water ways can make.

Another April Morning

Another April morning,
the poet says,
And here we are again,
as if April mornings have become
routine, commonplace,
just another thing to take for granted,
and yet, in a lifetime of 70 years,
you'll only have a little more
than 2000 April mornings,
about the same number of times
you'll visit the bathroom in a year,
the number of steps
it takes to walk a mile,
the number of texts
you'll get in a month,
breaths you'll take in two hours,
heartbeats you'll feel
in a quarter of that.

Can that possibly be enough
mornings to feel such a season of opening,
of budding out and coming back,
of fresh starts and colored wings,
bright forms and softly warbling things,
of air that makes your breath deepen,
your feet walk further,
you heart beat with the strength
of anything renewed?

Coffee During Covid

It's not the same, of course.
Students don't unpack at the table,
linger for hours, doing homework,
sipping on a single almond milk latte;
friends don't gather around,
sharing stories, getting refills,
trying Guatemalan, Costa Rican,
West Java Siliwangi.
The shop doesn't bustle
with the hustle of a steady flow,
drip or press, constant espress.
More a slow come and go
of customers, you already know
and knew would show no matter
the long distress of lasting woe.

Still, when you feel the chill
of autumn's coming on,
in a time of greater solitude,
lesser solace, uncertain hope,
a cup of coffee in the quiet cold
of morning can be a breath
of calm reassurance,
can feel something
like sudden comfort,
Dark Bliss, Cup of Joy,
Glorious Morning.

Reclamation

Having seen the transformation of one
rundown furniture plant into expensive
restaurant, brewery, boutique shops
for clothes and frozen yogurt, and noticing
the ongoing cleaning out of another,
and knowing it had already happened with my life,
education and divorce and writing
redeeming what had once been worthless,
I couldn't help but wonder how much
could be achieved with any body
nearly worn out, teeth straightened
with invisalign, eyes fixed by laser,
gut restored with probiotics,
foot pain eliminated by the Strassburg Sock,

but then even after rejuvenation,
even among the young, it's not always
pretty, not always full of grace,
the crude, oil-stained nuts and bolts
of life, the unphotogenic face,
a bad day that keeps getting worse,
walls that don't line up, some bricks
uneven, some not quite the right size,
and that's what the mortar's for,
the gray areas of tolerance,
forgiveness, understanding,
empathetic appreciation of things
being left imperfect, only as good
as we can stand to make them be.

What's Wrong with Super Powers

If I were a superhero, my name would be The Finder.
It's something I've always been good at.
Keys, cellphones, glasses, especially reading glasses,
all the things people commonly misplace,
or can't see when they're not wearing their glasses.

Or maybe I would be The Whistler,
or Whistler's Mother's Son for fun,
WMS for short, because I whistle all the time,
and I'm pretty good at it, although half the time
I can't tell you the name of the song
I'm whistling, just something I got in my head,
sometimes even a song I don't like,
Barry Manilow's "Copa Cabana" or that
Pina Colada song they always play at beach resorts.

My daughter says I would be The Riler
because I'm good at getting people riled up
about things, issues, ideas, perceived wrongs,
or just practical jokes, sarcasm,
pretended misunderstandings,
the sort of thing that's funny to 8 year olds
but is just called "Dad" jokes by everyone else.

I'm not sure I would want any of the usual
superhuman powers, flight, invisibility,
telekinesis, and definitely not mind reading.
They all seem to have inherent issues:
landing, being pervy, breaking things,
and all that noise, not to mention no surprises,

and everyone always wanting you to do tricks.

Maybe something less spectacular would be okay,
The Soother, or Calm Things Down Guy,
Recommend the Right Book Man, or The Alliterator.
But even those seem fraught with possibilities
for misuse, misunderstanding, misinterpretation
leading to mischief, misery, or mundane misfortune.
Maybe it's best I stick with what I know.
After all, I've always found finding
about as useful a skill as any I might manage.

WITH

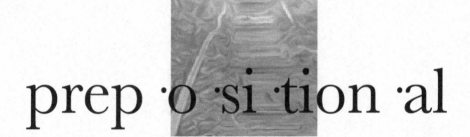

prep ·o ·si ·tion ·al

Common Ground

My brother has never kept a single lake,
a single lost grave to himself.
Always he calls, then waits until I
can come, lets me lead the way,
find it like the first time,
proclaiming the names I know, the shapes
of bird and stone, cloud and tree.

Once in the same day I saw
a kestrel, a mantis, an arrowhead
and took it as a sign, though since
I have seen each in their own days
and miles away from each other.

I do not believe God will bend
to kiss this mouth. I do not believe
the wine will turn to blood. But something
knows the moment of sunflower,
the time of crow's open wing,
the span of moss growing on rock,
and water washing it away.

In the pictures I remember, there is you
letting me stand on the fallen tree
as if it were mine. There is you
letting my arm rest on top of yours
around our mother. There is you
lifting me up to the limb I couldn't reach.

This is the faith I've wanted, to know
that even now we are capable of such
sacrifice, such willingness to love.

With

as if we were young
and knew what the future would hold;
as if we were in a new place
feeling all the anxious anticipation
of being in a new place;
as if nothing we could imagine
could not be real;
as if no one could have it better;
as if we would always be
what we always wanted;
as if there were no rules, or expectations;
as if we had all the answers
and the answers didn't matter;
as if we really believed we could do no wrong;

as if nothing could come between us;
as if no fall were possible
and nothing could ever be lost;
as if we had all the time in the world
because even death was too unreal to consider;
as if we could always get back
to how we used to be;
as if we were on a peaceful stroll
and the sky could not be more beautiful
and the temperature was perfect
and our hands met like strangers
and the world was blind around us
and soft music played from distant backyards
and we could smell camellias blooming in the dark.

we planted saplings
waited years to hear rain play
its music of leaves

            all the fallen
            gathered, a girl throws herself
            into leaves

Until

Expression of continued existence,
unchanged, or
anticipation of what
might end or yet be,
expectation of then,
ever promised ambition,
hope, the never-quite-there,
never-given-up-on.

I say, promise, pledge until--
until the last leaf falls,
trees refuse to bud,
buds refuse to flower,
flowers refuse
the intimations of bees,
directive of spring's unfolding,

until rainbows burn
to black, stars, heavy
with wishes, fall to the ground,
all lights go down on their own
accord and the unbearable
seriousness of gravity,

until the me of me,
the you of you alchemize
ourselves back to so much
water, carbon, calcium,
even until these dissolve
to nothing that can be named,

until every living thing
reveals the face of God
kept curled inside for centuries,
and the mouth of that face
says *No more.*

Setting the Stage

Sawyer at seven believes fairies
visit her room at night,
watch over her, bring her luck.
She attracted one with a locket,
a silver spoon, circle of stones.
She calls her *Amaryllis,* leaves her
oatmeal and honey, water in a pretty cup
for bathing her babies, flowers to dry them.

When she's older it will be important
that she knows the truth about things
both real and fantastic.
But for now, while she sleeps,
I'll keep pulling petals apart
and spreading them around her room.

Naming the Stars

At two you already knew
the awesome power of stars,
stood on toe tips to point,
reach, touch, pull them to you,
expressed amazement
when they disappeared
behind trees, joy
when they appeared again,
said you knew they would come back
for you to hold.

A decade later you float
through darkness, one among millions,
stringing together backyard
constellations faster
than my eyes can see
the possibilities you create,
gathering them in jars,
each one named
in defiance of loss
or the tyranny of infinity.

Refusing Loss

She turns over in bed.
Her hair gets in my mouth.
It's not as bad as you might think.
After lovemaking, few things are,
and so my life has been
since we first began together.

I lean close and whisper into darkness.
I'm sorry for every time I've come up short
of being the man you've wanted me to be.
I take back every cross word I've uttered,
every time I've said you were wrong
or let anything matter more than you.

O fading, familiar body beside me,
I would give up everything to prolong
what we have together.
I would swallow each strand
of this hair and more to purchase
even one more minute like this one.

Relativity

You tell me you can't trust what I say,
that I lie about your hair, the dress,
the way your eyes are still as bright
as the sea, your face as lovely as day,
your body the only one I think of
when my body yearns to be touched.
I tell you there is more than one truth.
My truth is always that I love you.
Let others tell you any other truth.

Barrier Islands

Three stories up on a rail at the south end
of Hatteras, I watch ferries come and go
taking their cargo of vacationers, one-day
diners, to more remote Ocracoke,
twenty miles of beach, sand, mosquitoes,
building up to hotel-studded Silver Lake,
artificial harbor said to be Edward Teach's
final hideaway before hanging, seabirds
and high tiders the only permanent residents.

On the other side, the ocean seems
to flow north, Gulfstream current
bringing enough warm water in which to swim,
double sandbar making it clearer
than I've ever seen this far north.
Sport fishermen cruise up and down
this coastline all day, hauling in
cobia, mackerel, drum. At night
I see their lights, singular in a sea
of darkness, sometimes hear voices
pitched just right to pierce
the constant roll of surf.

None of us leave much of a mark

on islands known to be temporary
themselves, migrating west,
shaped and reshaped by blue-green
waters of the Atlantic, patrolled
by timeless squads of gull
and tern, grackle and skimmer.
Footprints are washed or blown away
by nightfall, words drowned in the wind
and waves, everything else
consumed by time or sea.

Breaking Morning

This ritual of coffee is an ancient gesture.
One half of a couple rises early,
prepares the beans, the filtered water,
remembers exactly how much sugar
or cream, even the preferred size
or style of the cup. The other is moved
by the sound of the spoon tapped against
the rim, an articulation of aroma.
The presentation: cup in up-turned palm,
steam rising as if to announce *This*
was made especially for you.
Odysseus approached Penelope this way,
half in apology, half to say
you're still the one I wish to see at first light.

despite everything
my grown-up son remains
amazed by life

Out

Out the window I watch
white-breasted nuthatches hop
heads down down
the tree beside our feeder.

You ask if they are the only birds
that trust themselves to go
head down like that.
Zoned out as I am

for a moment, my face full
of wonder, I don't hear you
and when I do and turn
to answer that all nuthatches

share this downward habit,
you have tuned out
and are on your phone watching
in a moment of ecstatic observation

a video a friend has sent you.
No one gets upset.
No one walks out wounded.
We know the world is full

of beautiful things we want
to see and share, and we know
that living together is what
makes such distraction possible.

Aging Love

You snore.
I snort.
Your hip hurts.
My hands ache.
You toss and turn
And get up to go to the bathroom.
I toss and turn
And wake up from crazy dreams.
Our nighttimes may not be
What they used to be,
And I will admit to sometimes
Wanting what we once had,
But nighttimes or daytimes
no matter what they become
I always want them to be with you.

prep ·o ·si ·tion ·al

/ˌprepəˈziSH(ə)n(ə)l/

THROUGH

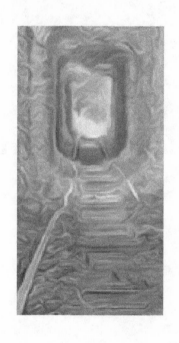

By

I love towns called Midway,
places defined only
by relativity to other places,
North Augusta, Ninety-Six, Due West.

Such prepositional location
appeals to me.
North of Boston.
South of Main.
Falls of the Neuse.

I think of Frost in the woods,
going on, keeping promises,
and I want to be known
for what I've lived
between, next to, by:
Sawyer's Daddy, teacher,
gardener, reader of poems.

Wild and Precious

In Memorium, Mary Oliver, 1/17/19

Seen at a distance this time of year
when trees are silhouettes
against a white sky
every shadow, I think,
must be a bird I'd like to identify,
waxwings, falcon, the largest of them
surely a beautiful hawk waiting
to chase a careless squirrel
across the yard and twice
around the trunk of the pecan tree,
rising on perfectly banked wings
so close it could almost reach out
and grasp the tuft of tail fur
dancing behind.

More often it turns out to be mistletoe,
nest, mere leftover leaves,
but even these speak
of life that was,
that will soon enough return,
and that truthfully always is.

Mary Oliver, the woman I've introduced
to more than 20 years of new students
as one of our greatest living poets,
died today,
but in view of trees, and birds,
and winter skies, and everything
that can be expressed in leaves,
it is impossible to think of her
as ever going away.

cold December sky
I gather blue
to sustain me

                              there are no answers
                              only the doing only
                              the yet to be done

Forward

My heroes are not those
who survive the horrors of war
anymore than they who survive

every day. Victors
of interior battles, they hold
their demons at bay, keep

the gun in the drawer,
knife on the table,
pills in the bottle,

continue to fight the good fight
against daily injustice, uncertainty,
decades of being degraded,

told they don't matter,
are less than, unworthy
of love, opportunity, fairness.

I love best those
who get up in the morning
no matter how bleak the prospect

of morning might be,
who stand up for themselves
or anyone else who needs it,

who continually, convincingly,
courageously,
push things forward.

Through

The old oak
has lost
more leaves
than most
has learned
to let
more light
shine through

Keeping Pace

I'm slowing down,
not because I have to,
not because the joints
of my bones take longer to bend,
not because rising from bed
I've become like a crane slowly
unfolding and lifting from water,
but because I've learned
how much everything likes
to be touched unhurriedly,
with careful intention, and because
the good enough job was never really
good enough, and more
was never better than good.

At the Reading

When I arrive, they number no more
than 10 or 12, mostly in couples,
a few alone, all chatting or checking
their phones. One or two look up
to take my measure, establish expectations,
the rest continue as they were.
My host says, *Don't worry; it's always
a late arriving crowd.* I reply,
*No problem. I've read to as few as two
and would do so again if necessary.*
She smiles, directs me to sit on stage,
turns her attention to a student
checking sound, pointing at the light booth.
More begin to drift in,
glance up at me. I return their looks,
nod, smile, mouth a hello,
shuffle through papers. The rows
begin to fill, 20, 30,
40, most with backpacks
and water bottles, one with a pillow.
After an introduction I begin,
oldest to newest, keep it mostly light,
tell stories that are easy to follow,
mix in a little humor, make a point
now and then. At the end
I invite questions. The usual.
Influences. Who they should read.
How I got started. Then,
the one with the pillow asks,
what I hope to achieve
by writing and reading poetry.

Not what I expected, I ramble

a moment, over making a difference,
saving something, poetry
its own reward, then it settles
in my head and I hear myself say,
Mostly I figure if I tell them enough
times, in enough different ways
that despite everything, the world
is a fine place to be and that they
can make it even better, then sooner
or later they'll have to believe it,
even if only a little.

The Lost Poems

I've grown so old, on occasion,
I lose poems, not poems by others.
I've lost those for years, decades even.
Poems of my own now, spoken
into my phone, written on napkins,
sent by email, then something happens,
and they're no longer there
when I'm ready to retrieve them,
hammer them out into what they could be,
what I imagined they would be
when I first started them.
I don't know how many I've lost.
I probably should, but I fear
I've lost that too. Still,
I feel there's at least a book's worth
of poems lying about somewhere
waiting for someone to find them.
If you do, please,
write them down in some place safe.
Keep them from obscurity.
Put your name on them.
It doesn't matter who gets the credit,
just that what they say gets heard.

Ever

I would not leave it willingly for anything,
although I know it's never easy
and so full of sadness it makes tracks
in our faces, so full of pain it wrecks
hands, back, neck, nothing
at times but disappointment, a constant
rerun of days, routines of labor
and failure, attempt and frustration,
only rarely coming out on top.
Yet, when I can no longer wrestle
with the demands of the day and win,
still, I would not leave it willingly.
Even set upright in the chair,
blanket across my lap with nothing
but sight left, or sound, or any
sensation along the length of my body,
or nothing but thought, even reduced
to carcass or compost, mere elements,
or rising again in the veins of limbs
I would not leave it willingly, or ever.

Nearing the end of my sentence

I grow desperate for more
time, more opportunity for meaning.
I grope about for a preposition,
conjunction, dangling participle. I grasp
for justification of just one more phrase,
through the gossamer backlit dress,
even a fragment, *a silhouette of bare thighs,*
hoping for a run-on, a bit of enjambment,
legs wrap around my waist
I am unable to resist. I wonder
what comes next, *descending towards oblivion,*
how painful the transition might be.
I long for a semi-colon, a dash,
parentheses, at least another comma.

prep·o·si·tion·al

/ˌprepəˈziSH(ə)n(ə)l/

All the Way Up to the Line
and
Beyond

1
From the first time
He said, "You can't,"
I knew my purpose
Was to prove him wrong.

2
And this is the way you play the game,
The only way, to win.
He drew a line in the sand
And dared me to cross,
And I crossed.

3
I have invented myself 50 times,
recycled possum and Papa,
teeth and hands,
the color red,
anything that might be called God,
and I do not tire of any of it.

4
Today I begin to see myself
as older, no longer a 14 year
mind in a 50-year body,
aware that power and prowess
now lie curled in soft places
before a fire and what remains
moves like smoke.
5

Every day I let my body recover
A little from the harm I do it,
the fall of most of it
always raising a little,
saving what must be spent.

6
Who has not knelt scared before the altar,
little eased by a promise of salvation
from him who made such necessary,
holy bully, trickster, inventor of Mafioso
insurance? Better to take our chances
without anticipation, prelude to disappointment.

7
Foot down, loathe to slow,
refusing to stop, believing
the line to be arbitrary,
impotent, only slightly
more than illusion.

8
After dark the sky
clears, and all the scraps
of clouds are illuminated
with moonlight and wet
with what lingers in air.

9
I am sure there is no other
place to go. I carry heaven
in my back pocket, in fingers'
soft touch, in the cups
of eyes. Who would dispense
with the joy of desire,
faint pleasure of need?

10

In front of, above,
next to, after,
inside, beyond,
all a gift of preposition.

11

Why worry of what will be
if not for persistence
of something like a soul,
if not for intuition
that this will always be
and you a part of it?

12

I am grateful for forgiveness,
for cloudy days, for birdsong
and edible roots, for second chances,
for hands, for sight, for learning to make.
I am grateful I never lost my hair,
that the students still come,
that words have never failed me.

13

As long as there are woods
it is worth the living.
As long as there is language
it is worth the living.
As long as there is breath
it is worth the living.
As long as there is the familiar of expectation
it is worth the living.

Used

I want to be used up by life,
all resources expended,
all reserves exhausted,
thistle picked clean,
river run dry.
I want to work to the last
minute at making and giving,
and take nothing with me.

After my last breath,
if there is anything left
unused, I'll feel I've failed,
and will only be saved by those
who need what I have
coming to carry it away.

Into

So Norman died, of course,
like everyone, but being
Norman, of course,
he couldn't die like everyone.
He couldn't die no
ordinary death.
He had to die
all over the place at once.
He had to die
all into things.
He had to spread himself out
like a warm day
and lie there like everyone
dying, slowly turning
into something else.

So he left his fingers
on the ground and they
turned into earthworms
and crawled away.
And he let his ears
fly free, the wings
they'd always wanted
to be. And he let his eyes
roll into the ocean
to become pearls
held tight in oysters'
clamped shut shells.
His hair spun itself
into spider webs
that stretch across your face.

His skull opened itself
for chipmunks and night things
to nest in. His face
became a flower with one eye
that winked open
in the morning, winked
closed at night.
His leg became a persimmon
branch, its unripe fruit
turning your mouth
inside out. His heart
hardened into stone.
His bones picked themselves up
and wandered to the river
and threw themselves in
and flowed downstream
until a beaver gathered them
together for his dam.
His lips turned into blades
of grass that whistle
with every breeze.
His arms transformed
into wild lime trees,
covered with spines
and yellow fruit,
inviting, forbidding,
finally at ease with contraries.
His tongue flew into the wind
and was never heard from again.
His skin had grown so thin
it easily changed into birchbark
and started peeling away.

And his hand,

his hard right hand
which never learned to hold
anything gently turned into
a leaf that held wind,
rain, sunlight upon it,
then let everything go.

cemetery rain –
even the stones
wear down

Epitaph

beneath this stone
is an old soldier
still
trying to be
all he can be,
made immortal
not by these words
destined to be
well-lichened and mossed
or by anything
he ever was
but by what
he yet may be,
given time and not
too much shade,
a blade of grass
a green root
a part of what
your boot stubs up.

Away

On the last day of the world
some pray, some cry, some
take whatever they never had,
most just eat chocolate.

On the last day of the world
people drive their cars
as fast as they can. My mother
finally sits down to rest.

On the last day of the world
the president is unavailable,
lovers are everywhere,
children play as if it were
the last day of the world,
at least one news broadcaster
continues to the very end.

On the last day of the world
there is a strange quiet in the air,
the leaves on the trees seem ready
to take wing, the birds have gone,
the sky is like a mouth
yawning.

On the last day of the world
the girl at the Dollar General
on Highway 16 puts everything
on sale, then walks out,
turns toward the river
and just keeps going.

About the Author

Scott Owens holds degrees from Ohio University, UNC Charlotte, and UNC Greensboro. He is Professor of Poetry at Lenoir Rhyne University, former editor of *Wild Goose Poetry Review* and *Southern Poetry Review*. He owns and operates Taste Full Beans Coffeehouse and Gallery and coordinates Poetry Hickory. He is the author of 17 collections of poetry and recipient of awards from the Academy of American Poets, the Pushcart Prize Anthology, the Next Generation/Indie Lit Awards, the North Carolina Writers Network, the North Carolina Poetry Society, and the Poetry Society of South Carolina. He has been featured in The Writer's Almanac seven times, and his articles about poetry have been featured frequently in *Poet's Market*.